T0167047

The Five Minute

Positive Focus
Daily Journal

The Five Minute

Positive Focus

Daily Journal

What You Think About...
You Bring About

Sandra Selby

BALBOA
PRESS

A DIVISION OF HAY HOUSE

Copyright © 2012 Sandra Selby

All rights reserved. No part of this book may be used or reproduced by
any means, graphic, electronic, or mechanical, including photocopying,
recording, taping or by any information storage retrieval system
without the written permission of the publisher except in the case
of brief quotations embodied in critical articles and reviews.

Library of Congress Control Number: 2012909492

ISBN: 978-1-4525-5109-8 (sc)
ISBN: 978-1-4525-5110-4 (hc)
ISBN: 978-1-4525-5108-1 (e)

Balboa Press books may be ordered through booksellers or by contacting:

Balboa Press
A Division of Hay House
1663 Liberty Drive
Bloomington, IN 47403
www.balboapress.com
1-(877) 407-4847

Because of the dynamic nature of the Internet, any web addresses or
links contained in this book may have changed since publication and may
no longer be valid. The views expressed in this work are solely those
of the author and do not necessarily reflect the views of the publisher,
and the publisher hereby disclaims any responsibility for them.

The author of this book does not dispense medical advice or
prescribe the use of any technique as a form of treatment for physical,
emotional, or medical problems without the advice of a physician,
either directly or indirectly. The intent of the author is only to offer
information of a general nature to help you in your quest for emotional
and spiritual well-being. In the event you use any of the information
in this book for yourself, which is your constitutional right, the author
and the publisher assume no responsibility for your actions.

Cover design, and all artwork in this book by Sandra Selby

Printed in the United States of America

Balboa Press rev. date: 9/212012

Acknowledgements

I was introduced to the Positive Focus concept thirty years ago during a very difficult time in my life. I was experiencing post partum depression and I could not see my way out of it. I am so grateful that I found a therapist who began using Creative Visualization techniques with me, followed by Affirmations and other concepts such as Positive Focus. At first I was hesitant to believe that it was possible to make a change in my reality by thinking differently, but results started to show otherwise. I began to take better care of myself and my family, I initiated some creative projects that had been neglected for many months, and I began seeking out new friends who believed in this same new positive fashion. To those friends and that dedicated therapist-thank YOU!

Thirty one years of gratitude to my husband Nick Selby who has encouraged and believed in me even when my faith in myself has faltered. You are a blessing to me.

A special 'shout out' to Dianne Bradley for joining me in my quest to find others who are positively oriented. We have participated in a wide variety of study groups over the years. I value your wisdom, insights…and your delightful sense of humor.

Many thanks to the Unity community and Unity minister Wendy Craig Purcell for encouraging me to seek the inner wisdom I knew to be true.

Big doses of gratitude go to Jane McAllen, manager of The Unity Center bookstore in San Diego. Jane prodded me for nearly a year to take on this project, as she recognized a need for just such a journal. Her vision helped make this a reality.

I thank the folks at Balboa Press for their guidance though the publishing process. Also, loads of appreciation to Breanna Peart for her expertise with graphic art.

Many blessings to my 'Focus' group who helped me to clarify the flow of the journal -Janet Gallegos, Patty Sommer, Annie Clopine, Kelly Dunn and Nancy Evans.

To Carol Nyhoff who guided me with her prayers, inspiration, encouragement and perfect wordings during the entire writing process-you are a treasure.

Lastly, to my daughter, Morgan, and son, Tyler- it is a heartfelt pleasure watching you on your own positive journeys…love to you both.

What You Think About...
You Bring About

I believe that each of us is born with unique gifts, talents, and burning desires... to help us to progress in this life and make a difference by sharing ourselves.

The mission of this journal is to help you *positively focus on what you WANT instead of what you don't want in your life. What you THINK ABOUT is what* you get MORE of. Wouldn't you like it to be MORE of what you WANT?

Every day, allow yourself a few minutes to fill in the five categories on a fresh journal page. Within just a few short weeks you will begin to notice that what you had written in your 'Divine Dreams and Desires' section has begun to manifest. Now you can add it to the 'What am I GRATEFUL for today?' section! It is a wonderful process to experience in such a visual way.

Every little step counts on the way to your progress and enlightenment. You will inspire others to do the same.

Most of all...have FUN with this process!

Namaste,
Sandra Selby

1

Positive Focus Journaling

How to get the most out of this process!

STEP ONE- What am I GRATEFUL for today?

Do not get too uptight over this. Write down whatever pops into your head. As positive manifestations begin to occur, remember to enter them in this section and in the next. You will be amazed at your progress after a few weeks of committing to focus just five minutes daily on the positive.

Example- My bed...my cat ...my kids...

STEP TWO- I ACKNOWLEDGE SUCCESSES in myself and others!

This section is very powerful. Many people are used to focusing on what they haven't accomplished instead of all the small and large steps that they have. As we acknowledge ourselves it helps to build self esteem and belief in our own progress. As we acknowledge others we expand our kindness and encouragement. These are wonderful ways to build our positive focus.

Example- I had a very productive day yesterday in my office. So happy that I 'intended' that for myself! My daughter is doing well in her new job!

STEP THREE- DIVINE DESIRES and DREAMS- What is my 'heart's desire'?

This area is meant to be a place for your dreams and desires of ALL sizes. We all have BIG dreams as well as everyday smaller desires. Put it all down, repeat them as often as you would like...or do a new one every day. I am focused on my work quite a bit, but as holidays or family issues arise, this is the area that I put down exactly what I would like to happen...or what I would like something to LOOK like when it is completed. This will take the emotionality out of it, and the fears. Imagine that it is 'a perfect world' and that you can have whatever you want...what would that be?

Example- I see myself at my perfect weight and size-healthy and energetic and fitting into beautiful clothes.

STEP FOUR- Picture DREAMS as ALREADY FULFILLED-How does that FEEL?

You will 'cement' your dream in your consciousness by tapping into the FEELING level. Describe your feelings in however much detail you can. FEELINGS are what actually draw your dreams and desires to you. No fear allowed-just pure joy. Trust in the Universe.

Example- I feel FABULOUS! So proud of myself! Smiling all over!! I feel HEALTHY and energetic-I can easily run up a staircase now without being winded! YAY!

STEP FIVE- POSITIVE INTENTION for TODAY- A Step toward my dreams!

This is your action step. You are putting your energy where your Dreams are... and the Universe will meet you tenfold. Make the step easy to handle and you may end up adding other steps to it. Do not let yourself get overwhelmed with HUGE assignments that stop the positive process before it has begun.

Example- I will investigate one healthy weight loss program today.

What am I GRATEFUL for today?

_____

_____

_____

_____

I ACKNOWLEDGE SUCCESSES in myself and others!

_____

_____

_____

_____

DIVINE DESIRES and DREAMS- What is my 'heart's desire'?

_____

_____

_____

_____

Picture your DREAMS as ALREADY FULFILLED-How does that FEEL?

_____

_____

_____

_____

POSITIVE INTENTION for TODAY- A Step toward my dreams!

_____

_____

_____

_____

What am I GRATEFUL for today?

_____
_____
_____
_____

I ACKNOWLEDGE SUCCESSES in myself and others!

_____
_____
_____
_____

DIVINE DESIRES and DREAMS- What is my 'heart's desire'?

_____
_____
_____
_____

Picture your DREAMS as ALREADY FULFILLED-How does that FEEL?

_____
_____
_____
_____

POSITIVE INTENTION for TODAY- A Step toward my dreams!

_____
_____
_____
_____

What am I GRATEFUL for today?

_____

_____

_____

_____

I ACKNOWLEDGE SUCCESSES in myself and others!

_____

_____

_____

_____

DIVINE DESIRES and DREAMS- What is my 'heart's desire'?

_____

_____

_____

_____

Picture your DREAMS as ALREADY FULFILLED-How does that FEEL?

_____

_____

_____

_____

POSITIVE INTENTION for TODAY- A Step toward my dreams!

_____

_____

_____

_____

What am I GRATEFUL for today?

_____
_____
_____
_____

I ACKNOWLEDGE SUCCESSES in myself and others!

_____
_____
_____
_____

DIVINE DESIRES and DREAMS- What is my 'heart's desire'?

_____
_____
_____
_____

Picture your DREAMS as ALREADY FULFILLED-How does that FEEL?

_____
_____
_____
_____

POSITIVE INTENTION for TODAY- A Step toward my dreams!

_____
_____
_____
_____

What am I GRATEFUL for today?

_____
_____
_____
_____

I ACKNOWLEDGE SUCCESSES in myself and others!

_____
_____
_____
_____

DIVINE DESIRES and DREAMS- What is my 'heart's desire'?

_____
_____
_____
_____

Picture your DREAMS as ALREADY FULFILLED-How does that FEEL?

_____
_____
_____
_____

POSITIVE INTENTION for TODAY- A Step toward my dreams!

_____
_____
_____
_____

What am I GRATEFUL for today?

_____
_____
_____
_____

I ACKNOWLEDGE SUCCESSES in myself and others!

_____
_____
_____
_____

DIVINE DESIRES and DREAMS- What is my 'heart's desire'?

_____
_____
_____
_____

Picture your DREAMS as ALREADY FULFILLED-How does that FEEL?

_____
_____
_____
_____

POSITIVE INTENTION for TODAY- A Step toward my dreams!

_____
_____
_____
_____

What am I GRATEFUL for today?

_____

_____

_____

_____

I ACKNOWLEDGE SUCCESSES in myself and others!

_____

_____

_____

_____

DIVINE DESIRES and DREAMS- What is my 'heart's desire'?

_____

_____

_____

_____

Picture your DREAMS as ALREADY FULFILLED-How does that FEEL?

_____

_____

_____

_____

POSITIVE INTENTION for TODAY- A Step toward my dreams!

_____

_____

_____

_____

What am I GRATEFUL for today?

_____
_____
_____
_____

I ACKNOWLEDGE SUCCESSES in myself and others!

_____
_____
_____
_____

DIVINE DESIRES and DREAMS- What is my 'heart's desire'?

_____
_____
_____
_____

Picture your DREAMS as ALREADY FULFILLED-How does that FEEL?

_____
_____
_____
_____

POSITIVE INTENTION for TODAY- A Step toward my dreams!

_____
_____
_____
_____

What am I GRATEFUL for today?   Date: _____

_____
_____
_____
_____

I ACKNOWLEDGE SUCCESSES in myself and others!

_____
_____
_____
_____

DIVINE DESIRES and DREAMS- What is my 'heart's desire'?

_____
_____
_____
_____

Picture your DREAMS as ALREADY FULFILLED-How does that FEEL?

_____
_____
_____
_____

POSITIVE INTENTION for TODAY- A Step toward my dreams!

_____
_____
_____
_____

What am I GRATEFUL for today?

_____

_____

_____

_____

I ACKNOWLEDGE SUCCESSES in myself and others!

_____

_____

_____

_____

DIVINE DESIRES and DREAMS- What is my 'heart's desire'?

_____

_____

_____

_____

Picture your DREAMS as ALREADY FULFILLED-How does that FEEL?

_____

_____

_____

_____

POSITIVE INTENTION for TODAY- A Step toward my dreams!

_____

_____

_____

_____

What am I GRATEFUL for today?   Date: _____

_____
_____
_____
_____

I ACKNOWLEDGE SUCCESSES in myself and others!

_____
_____
_____
_____

DIVINE DESIRES and DREAMS- What is my 'heart's desire'?

_____
_____
_____
_____

Picture your DREAMS as ALREADY FULFILLED-How does that FEEL?

_____
_____
_____
_____

POSITIVE INTENTION for TODAY- A Step toward my dreams!

_____
_____
_____
_____

What am I GRATEFUL for today?

_____
_____
_____
_____

I ACKNOWLEDGE SUCCESSES in myself and others!

_____
_____
_____
_____

DIVINE DESIRES and DREAMS- What is my 'heart's desire'?

_____
_____
_____
_____

Picture your DREAMS as ALREADY FULFILLED-How does that FEEL?

_____
_____
_____
_____

POSITIVE INTENTION for TODAY- A Step toward my dreams!

_____
_____
_____
_____

What am I GRATEFUL for today?

Date: _____

_____
_____
_____
_____

I ACKNOWLEDGE SUCCESSES in myself and others!

_____
_____
_____
_____

DIVINE DESIRES and DREAMS- What is my 'heart's desire'?

_____
_____
_____
_____

Picture your DREAMS as ALREADY FULFILLED-How does that FEEL?

_____
_____
_____
_____

POSITIVE INTENTION for TODAY- A Step toward my dreams!

_____
_____
_____
_____

What am I GRATEFUL for today?

_____
_____
_____
_____

I ACKNOWLEDGE SUCCESSES in myself and others!

_____
_____
_____
_____

DIVINE DESIRES and DREAMS- What is my 'heart's desire'?

_____
_____
_____
_____

Picture your DREAMS as ALREADY FULFILLED-How does that FEEL?

_____
_____
_____
_____

POSITIVE INTENTION for TODAY- A Step toward my dreams!

_____
_____
_____
_____

What am I GRATEFUL for today?

Date: _____

_____
_____
_____
_____

I ACKNOWLEDGE SUCCESSES in myself and others!

_____
_____
_____
_____

DIVINE DESIRES and DREAMS- What is my 'heart's desire'?

_____
_____
_____
_____

Picture your DREAMS as ALREADY FULFILLED-How does that FEEL?

_____
_____
_____
_____

POSITIVE INTENTION for TODAY- A Step toward my dreams!

_____
_____
_____
_____

What am I GRATEFUL for today?

_____
_____
_____
_____

I ACKNOWLEDGE SUCCESSES in myself and others!

_____
_____
_____
_____

DIVINE DESIRES and DREAMS- What is my 'heart's desire'?

_____
_____
_____
_____

Picture your DREAMS as ALREADY FULFILLED-How does that FEEL?

_____
_____
_____
_____

POSITIVE INTENTION for TODAY- A Step toward my dreams!

_____
_____
_____
_____

What am I GRATEFUL for today?

_____

_____

_____

_____

I ACKNOWLEDGE SUCCESSES in myself and others!

_____

_____

_____

_____

DIVINE DESIRES and DREAMS- What is my 'heart's desire'?

_____

_____

_____

_____

Picture your DREAMS as ALREADY FULFILLED-How does that FEEL?

_____

_____

_____

_____

POSITIVE INTENTION for TODAY- A Step toward my dreams!

_____

_____

_____

_____

What am I GRATEFUL for today?

_____
_____
_____
_____

I ACKNOWLEDGE SUCCESSES in myself and others!

_____
_____
_____
_____

DIVINE DESIRES and DREAMS- What is my 'heart's desire'?

_____
_____
_____
_____

Picture your DREAMS as ALREADY FULFILLED-How does that FEEL?

_____
_____
_____
_____

POSITIVE INTENTION for TODAY- A Step toward my dreams!

_____
_____
_____
_____

What am I GRATEFUL for today?

_____

_____

_____

_____

I ACKNOWLEDGE SUCCESSES in myself and others!

_____

_____

_____

_____

DIVINE DESIRES and DREAMS- What is my 'heart's desire'?

_____

_____

_____

_____

Picture your DREAMS as ALREADY FULFILLED-How does that FEEL?

_____

_____

_____

_____

POSITIVE INTENTION for TODAY- A Step toward my dreams!

_____

_____

_____

_____

What am I GRATEFUL for today?

_____
_____
_____
_____

I ACKNOWLEDGE SUCCESSES in myself and others!

_____
_____
_____
_____

DIVINE DESIRES and DREAMS- What is my 'heart's desire'?

_____
_____
_____
_____

Picture your DREAMS as ALREADY FULFILLED-How does that FEEL?

_____
_____
_____
_____

POSITIVE INTENTION for TODAY- A Step toward my dreams!

_____
_____
_____
_____

What am I GRATEFUL for today?

_____
_____
_____
_____

I ACKNOWLEDGE SUCCESSES in myself and others!

_____
_____
_____
_____

DIVINE DESIRES and DREAMS- What is my 'heart's desire'?

_____
_____
_____
_____

Picture your DREAMS as ALREADY FULFILLED-How does that FEEL?

_____
_____
_____
_____

POSITIVE INTENTION for TODAY- A Step toward my dreams!

_____
_____
_____
_____

What am I GRATEFUL for today?

_____
_____
_____
_____

I ACKNOWLEDGE SUCCESSES in myself and others!

_____
_____
_____
_____

DIVINE DESIRES and DREAMS- What is my 'heart's desire'?

_____
_____
_____
_____

Picture your DREAMS as ALREADY FULFILLED-How does that FEEL?

_____
_____
_____
_____

POSITIVE INTENTION for TODAY- A Step toward my dreams!

_____
_____
_____
_____

What am I GRATEFUL for today?   Date: _____

_____
_____
_____
_____

I ACKNOWLEDGE SUCCESSES in myself and others!

_____
_____
_____
_____

DIVINE DESIRES and DREAMS- What is my 'heart's desire'?

_____
_____
_____
_____

Picture your DREAMS as ALREADY FULFILLED-How does that FEEL?

_____
_____
_____
_____

POSITIVE INTENTION for TODAY- A Step toward my dreams!

_____
_____
_____
_____

What am I GRATEFUL for today?

_____

_____

_____

_____

I ACKNOWLEDGE SUCCESSES in myself and others!

_____

_____

_____

_____

DIVINE DESIRES and DREAMS- What is my 'heart's desire'?

_____

_____

_____

_____

Picture your DREAMS as ALREADY FULFILLED-How does that FEEL?

_____

_____

_____

_____

POSITIVE INTENTION for TODAY- A Step toward my dreams!

_____

_____

_____

_____

What am I GRATEFUL for today?

_____
_____
_____
_____

I ACKNOWLEDGE SUCCESSES in myself and others!

_____
_____
_____
_____

DIVINE DESIRES and DREAMS- What is my 'heart's desire'?

_____
_____
_____
_____

Picture your DREAMS as ALREADY FULFILLED-How does that FEEL?

_____
_____
_____
_____

POSITIVE INTENTION for TODAY- A Step toward my dreams!

_____
_____
_____
_____

What am I GRATEFUL for today?

_____
_____
_____
_____

I ACKNOWLEDGE SUCCESSES in myself and others!

_____
_____
_____
_____

DIVINE DESIRES and DREAMS- What is my 'heart's desire'?

_____
_____
_____
_____

Picture your DREAMS as ALREADY FULFILLED-How does that FEEL?

_____
_____
_____
_____

POSITIVE INTENTION for TODAY- A Step toward my dreams!

_____
_____
_____
_____

What am I GRATEFUL for today?

_____
_____
_____
_____

I ACKNOWLEDGE SUCCESSES in myself and others!

_____
_____
_____
_____

DIVINE DESIRES and DREAMS- What is my 'heart's desire'?

_____
_____
_____
_____

Picture your DREAMS as ALREADY FULFILLED-How does that FEEL?

_____
_____
_____
_____

POSITIVE INTENTION for TODAY- A Step toward my dreams!

_____
_____
_____
_____

What am I GRATEFUL for today?

_____
_____
_____
_____

I ACKNOWLEDGE SUCCESSES in myself and others!

_____
_____
_____
_____

DIVINE DESIRES and DREAMS- What is my 'heart's desire'?

_____
_____
_____
_____

Picture your DREAMS as ALREADY FULFILLED-How does that FEEL?

_____
_____
_____
_____

POSITIVE INTENTION for TODAY- A Step toward my dreams!

_____
_____
_____
_____

What am I GRATEFUL for today?

Date: _____

_____
_____
_____
_____

I ACKNOWLEDGE SUCCESSES in myself and others!

_____
_____
_____
_____

DIVINE DESIRES and DREAMS- What is my 'heart's desire'?

_____
_____
_____
_____

Picture your DREAMS as ALREADY FULFILLED-How does that FEEL?

_____
_____
_____
_____

POSITIVE INTENTION for TODAY- A Step toward my dreams!

_____
_____
_____
_____

What am I GRATEFUL for today?

_____
_____
_____
_____

I ACKNOWLEDGE SUCCESSES in myself and others!

_____
_____
_____
_____

DIVINE DESIRES and DREAMS- What is my 'heart's desire'?

_____
_____
_____
_____

Picture your DREAMS as ALREADY FULFILLED-How does that FEEL?

_____
_____
_____
_____

POSITIVE INTENTION for TODAY- A Step toward my dreams!

_____
_____
_____
_____

What am I GRATEFUL for today?

_____
_____
_____
_____

I ACKNOWLEDGE SUCCESSES in myself and others!

_____
_____
_____
_____

DIVINE DESIRES and DREAMS- What is my 'heart's desire'?

_____
_____
_____
_____

Picture your DREAMS as ALREADY FULFILLED-How does that FEEL?

_____
_____
_____
_____

POSITIVE INTENTION for TODAY- A Step toward my dreams!

_____
_____
_____
_____

What am I GRATEFUL for today?

_____
_____
_____
_____

I ACKNOWLEDGE SUCCESSES in myself and others!

_____
_____
_____
_____

DIVINE DESIRES and DREAMS- What is my 'heart's desire'?

_____
_____
_____
_____

Picture your DREAMS as ALREADY FULFILLED-How does that FEEL?

_____
_____
_____
_____

POSITIVE INTENTION for TODAY- A Step toward my dreams!

_____
_____
_____
_____

What am I GRATEFUL for today?

Date: _____

_____
_____
_____
_____

I ACKNOWLEDGE SUCCESSES in myself and others!

_____
_____
_____
_____

DIVINE DESIRES and DREAMS- What is my 'heart's desire'?

_____
_____
_____
_____

Picture your DREAMS as ALREADY FULFILLED-How does that FEEL?

_____
_____
_____
_____

POSITIVE INTENTION for TODAY- A Step toward my dreams!

_____
_____
_____
_____

What am I GRATEFUL for today?

_____

_____

_____

_____

I ACKNOWLEDGE SUCCESSES in myself and others!

_____

_____

_____

_____

DIVINE DESIRES and DREAMS- What is my 'heart's desire'?

_____

_____

_____

_____

Picture your DREAMS as ALREADY FULFILLED-How does that FEEL?

_____

_____

_____

_____

POSITIVE INTENTION for TODAY- A Step toward my dreams!

_____

_____

_____

_____

What am I GRATEFUL for today?

Date: _____

I ACKNOWLEDGE SUCCESSES in myself and others!

_____
_____
_____
_____

DIVINE DESIRES and DREAMS- What is my 'heart's desire'?

_____
_____
_____
_____

Picture your DREAMS as ALREADY FULFILLED-How does that FEEL?

_____
_____
_____
_____

POSITIVE INTENTION for TODAY- A Step toward my dreams!

_____
_____
_____
_____

What am I GRATEFUL for today?

_____

_____

_____

_____

I ACKNOWLEDGE SUCCESSES in myself and others!

_____

_____

_____

_____

DIVINE DESIRES and DREAMS- What is my 'heart's desire'?

_____

_____

_____

_____

Picture your DREAMS as ALREADY FULFILLED-How does that FEEL?

_____

_____

_____

_____

POSITIVE INTENTION for TODAY- A Step toward my dreams!

_____

_____

_____

_____

What am I GRATEFUL for today?

_____

_____

_____

_____

I ACKNOWLEDGE SUCCESSES in myself and others!

_____

_____

_____

_____

DIVINE DESIRES and DREAMS- What is my 'heart's desire'?

_____

_____

_____

_____

Picture your DREAMS as ALREADY FULFILLED-How does that FEEL?

_____

_____

_____

_____

POSITIVE INTENTION for TODAY- A Step toward my dreams!

_____

_____

_____

_____

What am I GRATEFUL for today?

_____

_____

_____

_____

I ACKNOWLEDGE SUCCESSES in myself and others!

_____

_____

_____

_____

DIVINE DESIRES and DREAMS- What is my 'heart's desire'?

_____

_____

_____

_____

Picture your DREAMS as ALREADY FULFILLED-How does that FEEL?

_____

_____

_____

_____

POSITIVE INTENTION for TODAY- A Step toward my dreams!

_____

_____

_____

_____

What am I GRATEFUL for today?

_____

_____

_____

_____

I ACKNOWLEDGE SUCCESSES in myself and others!

_____

_____

_____

_____

DIVINE DESIRES and DREAMS- What is my 'heart's desire'?

_____

_____

_____

_____

Picture your DREAMS as ALREADY FULFILLED-How does that FEEL?

_____

_____

_____

_____

POSITIVE INTENTION for TODAY- A Step toward my dreams!

_____

_____

_____

_____

What am I GRATEFUL for today?

_____
_____
_____
_____

I ACKNOWLEDGE SUCCESSES in myself and others!

_____
_____
_____
_____

DIVINE DESIRES and DREAMS- What is my 'heart's desire'?

_____
_____
_____
_____

Picture your DREAMS as ALREADY FULFILLED-How does that FEEL?

_____
_____
_____
_____

POSITIVE INTENTION for TODAY- A Step toward my dreams!

_____
_____
_____
_____

What am I GRATEFUL for today?

_____

_____

_____

_____

I ACKNOWLEDGE SUCCESSES in myself and others!

_____

_____

_____

_____

DIVINE DESIRES and DREAMS- What is my 'heart's desire'?

_____

_____

_____

_____

Picture your DREAMS as ALREADY FULFILLED-How does that FEEL?

_____

_____

_____

_____

POSITIVE INTENTION for TODAY- A Step toward my dreams!

_____

_____

_____

_____

What am I GRATEFUL for today?

_____
_____
_____
_____

I ACKNOWLEDGE SUCCESSES in myself and others!

_____
_____
_____
_____

DIVINE DESIRES and DREAMS- What is my 'heart's desire'?

_____
_____
_____
_____

Picture your DREAMS as ALREADY FULFILLED-How does that FEEL?

_____
_____
_____
_____

POSITIVE INTENTION for TODAY- A Step toward my dreams!

_____
_____
_____
_____

What am I GRATEFUL for today?

_____

_____

_____

_____

I ACKNOWLEDGE SUCCESSES in myself and others!

_____

_____

_____

_____

DIVINE DESIRES and DREAMS- What is my 'heart's desire'?

_____

_____

_____

_____

Picture your DREAMS as ALREADY FULFILLED-How does that FEEL?

_____

_____

_____

_____

POSITIVE INTENTION for TODAY- A Step toward my dreams!

_____

_____

_____

_____

What am I GRATEFUL for today?   Date: _____

_____
_____
_____
_____

I ACKNOWLEDGE SUCCESSES in myself and others!

_____
_____
_____
_____

DIVINE DESIRES and DREAMS- What is my 'heart's desire'?

_____
_____
_____
_____

Picture your DREAMS as ALREADY FULFILLED-How does that FEEL?

_____
_____
_____
_____

POSITIVE INTENTION for TODAY- A Step toward my dreams!

_____
_____
_____
_____

What am I GRATEFUL for today?

_____

_____
_____
_____
_____

I ACKNOWLEDGE SUCCESSES in myself and others!

_____
_____
_____
_____

DIVINE DESIRES and DREAMS- What is my 'heart's desire'?

_____
_____
_____
_____

Picture your DREAMS as ALREADY FULFILLED-How does that FEEL?

_____
_____
_____
_____

POSITIVE INTENTION for TODAY- A Step toward my dreams!

_____
_____
_____
_____

What am I GRATEFUL for today?

_____
_____
_____
_____

I ACKNOWLEDGE SUCCESSES in myself and others!

_____
_____
_____
_____

DIVINE DESIRES and DREAMS- What is my 'heart's desire'?

_____
_____
_____
_____

Picture your DREAMS as ALREADY FULFILLED-How does that FEEL?

_____
_____
_____
_____

POSITIVE INTENTION for TODAY- A Step toward my dreams!

_____
_____
_____
_____

What am I GRATEFUL for today?

_____
_____
_____
_____

I ACKNOWLEDGE SUCCESSES in myself and others!

_____
_____
_____
_____

DIVINE DESIRES and DREAMS- What is my 'heart's desire'?

_____
_____
_____
_____

Picture your DREAMS as ALREADY FULFILLED-How does that FEEL?

_____
_____
_____
_____

POSITIVE INTENTION for TODAY- A Step toward my dreams!

_____
_____
_____
_____

What am I GRATEFUL for today?

_____
_____
_____
_____

I ACKNOWLEDGE SUCCESSES in myself and others!

_____
_____
_____
_____

DIVINE DESIRES and DREAMS- What is my 'heart's desire'?

_____
_____
_____
_____

Picture your DREAMS as ALREADY FULFILLED-How does that FEEL?

_____
_____
_____
_____

POSITIVE INTENTION for TODAY- A Step toward my dreams!

_____
_____
_____
_____

What am I GRATEFUL for today?

_____

_____

_____

_____

I ACKNOWLEDGE SUCCESSES in myself and others!

_____

_____

_____

_____

DIVINE DESIRES and DREAMS- What is my 'heart's desire'?

_____

_____

_____

_____

Picture your DREAMS as ALREADY FULFILLED-How does that FEEL?

_____

_____

_____

_____

POSITIVE INTENTION for TODAY- A Step toward my dreams!

_____

_____

_____

_____

What am I GRATEFUL for today?

_____

_____

_____

_____

I ACKNOWLEDGE SUCCESSES in myself and others!

_____

_____

_____

_____

DIVINE DESIRES and DREAMS- What is my 'heart's desire'?

_____

_____

_____

_____

Picture your DREAMS as ALREADY FULFILLED-How does that FEEL?

_____

_____

_____

_____

POSITIVE INTENTION for TODAY- A Step toward my dreams!

_____

_____

_____

_____

What am I GRATEFUL for today?

_____
_____
_____
_____

I ACKNOWLEDGE SUCCESSES in myself and others!

_____
_____
_____
_____

DIVINE DESIRES and DREAMS- What is my 'heart's desire'?

_____
_____
_____
_____

Picture your DREAMS as ALREADY FULFILLED-How does that FEEL?

_____
_____
_____
_____

POSITIVE INTENTION for TODAY- A Step toward my dreams!

_____
_____
_____
_____

What am I GRATEFUL for today?

_____
_____
_____
_____

I ACKNOWLEDGE SUCCESSES in myself and others!

_____
_____
_____
_____

DIVINE DESIRES and DREAMS- What is my 'heart's desire'?

_____
_____
_____
_____

Picture your DREAMS as ALREADY FULFILLED-How does that FEEL?

_____
_____
_____
_____

POSITIVE INTENTION for TODAY- A Step toward my dreams!

_____
_____
_____
_____

What am I GRATEFUL for today?

_____
_____
_____
_____

I ACKNOWLEDGE SUCCESSES in myself and others!

_____
_____
_____
_____

DIVINE DESIRES and DREAMS- What is my 'heart's desire'?

_____
_____
_____
_____

Picture your DREAMS as ALREADY FULFILLED-How does that FEEL?

_____
_____
_____
_____

POSITIVE INTENTION for TODAY- A Step toward my dreams!

_____
_____
_____
_____

What am I GRATEFUL for today?

_____

_____

_____

_____

I ACKNOWLEDGE SUCCESSES in myself and others!

_____

_____

_____

_____

DIVINE DESIRES and DREAMS- What is my 'heart's desire'?

_____

_____

_____

_____

Picture your DREAMS as ALREADY FULFILLED-How does that FEEL?

_____

_____

_____

_____

POSITIVE INTENTION for TODAY- A Step toward my dreams!

_____

_____

_____

_____

What am I GRATEFUL for today?

_____

_____

_____

_____

I ACKNOWLEDGE SUCCESSES in myself and others!

_____

_____

_____

_____

DIVINE DESIRES and DREAMS- What is my 'heart's desire'?

_____

_____

_____

_____

Picture your DREAMS as ALREADY FULFILLED-How does that FEEL?

_____

_____

_____

_____

POSITIVE INTENTION for TODAY- A Step toward my dreams!

_____

_____

_____

_____

What am I GRATEFUL for today?

_____
_____
_____
_____

I ACKNOWLEDGE SUCCESSES in myself and others!

_____
_____
_____
_____

DIVINE DESIRES and DREAMS- What is my 'heart's desire'?

_____
_____
_____
_____

Picture your DREAMS as ALREADY FULFILLED-How does that FEEL?

_____
_____
_____
_____

POSITIVE INTENTION for TODAY- A Step toward my dreams!

_____
_____
_____
_____

What am I GRATEFUL for today?

_____
_____
_____
_____

I ACKNOWLEDGE SUCCESSES in myself and others!

_____
_____
_____
_____

DIVINE DESIRES and DREAMS- What is my 'heart's desire'?

_____
_____
_____
_____

Picture your DREAMS as ALREADY FULFILLED-How does that FEEL?

_____
_____
_____
_____

POSITIVE INTENTION for TODAY- A Step toward my dreams!

_____
_____
_____
_____

What am I GRATEFUL for today?

_____

_____

_____

_____

I ACKNOWLEDGE SUCCESSES in myself and others!

_____

_____

_____

_____

DIVINE DESIRES and DREAMS- What is my 'heart's desire'?

_____

_____

_____

_____

Picture your DREAMS as ALREADY FULFILLED-How does that FEEL?

_____

_____

_____

_____

POSITIVE INTENTION for TODAY- A Step toward my dreams!

_____

_____

_____

_____

What am I GRATEFUL for today?

_____
_____
_____
_____

I ACKNOWLEDGE SUCCESSES in myself and others!

_____
_____
_____
_____

DIVINE DESIRES and DREAMS- What is my 'heart's desire'?

_____
_____
_____
_____

Picture your DREAMS as ALREADY FULFILLED-How does that FEEL?

_____
_____
_____
_____

POSITIVE INTENTION for TODAY- A Step toward my dreams!

_____
_____
_____
_____

What am I GRATEFUL for today?

_____
_____
_____
_____

I ACKNOWLEDGE SUCCESSES in myself and others!

_____
_____
_____
_____

DIVINE DESIRES and DREAMS- What is my 'heart's desire'?

_____
_____
_____
_____

Picture your DREAMS as ALREADY FULFILLED-How does that FEEL?

_____
_____
_____
_____

POSITIVE INTENTION for TODAY- A Step toward my dreams!

_____
_____
_____
_____

What am I GRATEFUL for today?

_____
_____
_____
_____

I ACKNOWLEDGE SUCCESSES in myself and others!

_____
_____
_____
_____

DIVINE DESIRES and DREAMS- What is my 'heart's desire'?

_____
_____
_____
_____

Picture your DREAMS as ALREADY FULFILLED-How does that FEEL?

_____
_____
_____
_____

POSITIVE INTENTION for TODAY- A Step toward my dreams!

_____
_____
_____
_____

What am I GRATEFUL for today?

_____
_____
_____
_____

I ACKNOWLEDGE SUCCESSES in myself and others!

_____
_____
_____
_____

DIVINE DESIRES and DREAMS- What is my 'heart's desire'?

_____
_____
_____
_____

Picture your DREAMS as ALREADY FULFILLED-How does that FEEL?

_____
_____
_____
_____

POSITIVE INTENTION for TODAY- A Step toward my dreams!

_____
_____
_____
_____

What am I GRATEFUL for today?

_____
_____
_____
_____

I ACKNOWLEDGE SUCCESSES in myself and others!

_____
_____
_____
_____

DIVINE DESIRES and DREAMS- What is my 'heart's desire'?

_____
_____
_____
_____

Picture your DREAMS as ALREADY FULFILLED-How does that FEEL?

_____
_____
_____
_____

POSITIVE INTENTION for TODAY- A Step toward my dreams!

_____
_____
_____
_____

What am I GRATEFUL for today?

_____

_____

_____

_____

I ACKNOWLEDGE SUCCESSES in myself and others!

_____

_____

_____

_____

DIVINE DESIRES and DREAMS- What is my 'heart's desire'?

_____

_____

_____

_____

Picture your DREAMS as ALREADY FULFILLED-How does that FEEL?

_____

_____

_____

_____

POSITIVE INTENTION for TODAY- A Step toward my dreams!

_____

_____

_____

_____

What am I GRATEFUL for today?

_____
_____
_____
_____

I ACKNOWLEDGE SUCCESSES in myself and others!

_____
_____
_____
_____

DIVINE DESIRES and DREAMS- What is my 'heart's desire'?

_____
_____
_____
_____

Picture your DREAMS as ALREADY FULFILLED-How does that FEEL?

_____
_____
_____
_____

POSITIVE INTENTION for TODAY- A Step toward my dreams!

_____
_____
_____
_____

What am I GRATEFUL for today?

_____
_____
_____
_____

I ACKNOWLEDGE SUCCESSES in myself and others!

_____
_____
_____
_____

DIVINE DESIRES and DREAMS- What is my 'heart's desire'?

_____
_____
_____
_____

Picture your DREAMS as ALREADY FULFILLED-How does that FEEL?

_____
_____
_____
_____

POSITIVE INTENTION for TODAY- A Step toward my dreams!

_____
_____
_____
_____

What am I GRATEFUL for today?

_____
_____
_____
_____

I ACKNOWLEDGE SUCCESSES in myself and others!

_____
_____
_____
_____

DIVINE DESIRES and DREAMS- What is my 'heart's desire'?

_____
_____
_____
_____

Picture your DREAMS as ALREADY FULFILLED-How does that FEEL?

_____
_____
_____
_____

POSITIVE INTENTION for TODAY- A Step toward my dreams!

_____
_____
_____
_____

What am I GRATEFUL for today?

_____
_____
_____
_____

I ACKNOWLEDGE SUCCESSES in myself and others!

_____
_____
_____
_____

DIVINE DESIRES and DREAMS- What is my 'heart's desire'?

_____
_____
_____
_____

Picture your DREAMS as ALREADY FULFILLED-How does that FEEL?

_____
_____
_____
_____

POSITIVE INTENTION for TODAY- A Step toward my dreams!

_____
_____
_____
_____

What am I GRATEFUL for today?

_____
_____
_____
_____

I ACKNOWLEDGE SUCCESSES in myself and others!

_____
_____
_____
_____

DIVINE DESIRES and DREAMS- What is my 'heart's desire'?

_____
_____
_____
_____

Picture your DREAMS as ALREADY FULFILLED-How does that FEEL?

_____
_____
_____
_____

POSITIVE INTENTION for TODAY- A Step toward my dreams!

_____
_____
_____
_____

What am I GRATEFUL for today?

_____
_____
_____
_____

I ACKNOWLEDGE SUCCESSES in myself and others!

_____
_____
_____
_____

DIVINE DESIRES and DREAMS- What is my 'heart's desire'?

_____
_____
_____
_____

Picture your DREAMS as ALREADY FULFILLED-How does that FEEL?

_____
_____
_____
_____

POSITIVE INTENTION for TODAY- A Step toward my dreams!

_____
_____
_____
_____

What am I GRATEFUL for today?

_____

_____

_____

_____

I ACKNOWLEDGE SUCCESSES in myself and others!

_____

_____

_____

_____

DIVINE DESIRES and DREAMS- What is my 'heart's desire'?

_____

_____

_____

_____

Picture your DREAMS as ALREADY FULFILLED-How does that FEEL?

_____

_____

_____

_____

POSITIVE INTENTION for TODAY- A Step toward my dreams!

_____

_____

_____

_____

What am I GRATEFUL for today?

_____
_____
_____
_____

I ACKNOWLEDGE SUCCESSES in myself and others!

_____
_____
_____
_____

DIVINE DESIRES and DREAMS- What is my 'heart's desire'?

_____
_____
_____
_____

Picture your DREAMS as ALREADY FULFILLED-How does that FEEL?

_____
_____
_____
_____

POSITIVE INTENTION for TODAY- A Step toward my dreams!

_____
_____
_____
_____

What am I GRATEFUL for today?

_____

_____

_____

_____

I ACKNOWLEDGE SUCCESSES in myself and others!

_____

_____

_____

_____

DIVINE DESIRES and DREAMS- What is my 'heart's desire'?

_____

_____

_____

_____

Picture your DREAMS as ALREADY FULFILLED-How does that FEEL?

_____

_____

_____

_____

POSITIVE INTENTION for TODAY- A Step toward my dreams!

_____

_____

_____

_____

What am I GRATEFUL for today?

_____
_____
_____
_____

I ACKNOWLEDGE SUCCESSES in myself and others!

_____
_____
_____
_____

DIVINE DESIRES and DREAMS- What is my 'heart's desire'?

_____
_____
_____
_____

Picture your DREAMS as ALREADY FULFILLED-How does that FEEL?

_____
_____
_____
_____

POSITIVE INTENTION for TODAY- A Step toward my dreams!

_____
_____
_____
_____

What am I GRATEFUL for today?

_____
_____
_____
_____

I ACKNOWLEDGE SUCCESSES in myself and others!

_____
_____
_____
_____

DIVINE DESIRES and DREAMS- What is my 'heart's desire'?

_____
_____
_____
_____

Picture your DREAMS as ALREADY FULFILLED-How does that FEEL?

_____
_____
_____
_____

POSITIVE INTENTION for TODAY- A Step toward my dreams!

_____
_____
_____
_____

What am I GRATEFUL for today?

_____
_____
_____
_____

I ACKNOWLEDGE SUCCESSES in myself and others!

_____
_____
_____
_____

DIVINE DESIRES and DREAMS- What is my 'heart's desire'?

_____
_____
_____
_____

Picture your DREAMS as ALREADY FULFILLED-How does that FEEL?

_____
_____
_____
_____

POSITIVE INTENTION for TODAY- A Step toward my dreams!

_____
_____
_____
_____

What am I GRATEFUL for today?

_____
_____
_____
_____

I ACKNOWLEDGE SUCCESSES in myself and others!

_____
_____
_____
_____

DIVINE DESIRES and DREAMS- What is my 'heart's desire'?

_____
_____
_____
_____

Picture your DREAMS as ALREADY FULFILLED-How does that FEEL?

_____
_____
_____
_____

POSITIVE INTENTION for TODAY- A Step toward my dreams!

_____
_____
_____
_____

What am I GRATEFUL for today?

_____
_____
_____
_____

I ACKNOWLEDGE SUCCESSES in myself and others!

_____
_____
_____
_____

DIVINE DESIRES and DREAMS- What is my 'heart's desire'?

_____
_____
_____
_____

Picture your DREAMS as ALREADY FULFILLED-How does that FEEL?

_____
_____
_____
_____

POSITIVE INTENTION for TODAY- A Step toward my dreams!

_____
_____
_____
_____

What am I GRATEFUL for today?

_____

_____

_____

_____

I ACKNOWLEDGE SUCCESSES in myself and others!

_____

_____

_____

_____

DIVINE DESIRES and DREAMS- What is my 'heart's desire'?

_____

_____

_____

_____

Picture your DREAMS as ALREADY FULFILLED-How does that FEEL?

_____

_____

_____

_____

POSITIVE INTENTION for TODAY- A Step toward my dreams!

_____

_____

_____

_____

What am I GRATEFUL for today?

_____
_____
_____
_____

I ACKNOWLEDGE SUCCESSES in myself and others!

_____
_____
_____
_____

DIVINE DESIRES and DREAMS- What is my 'heart's desire'?

_____
_____
_____
_____

Picture your DREAMS as ALREADY FULFILLED-How does that FEEL?

_____
_____
_____
_____

POSITIVE INTENTION for TODAY- A Step toward my dreams!

_____
_____
_____
_____

What am I GRATEFUL for today?

_____
_____
_____
_____

I ACKNOWLEDGE SUCCESSES in myself and others!

_____
_____
_____
_____

DIVINE DESIRES and DREAMS- What is my 'heart's desire'?

_____
_____
_____
_____

Picture your DREAMS as ALREADY FULFILLED-How does that FEEL?

_____
_____
_____
_____

POSITIVE INTENTION for TODAY- A Step toward my dreams!

_____
_____
_____
_____

What am I GRATEFUL for today?

_____
_____
_____
_____

I ACKNOWLEDGE SUCCESSES in myself and others!

_____
_____
_____
_____

DIVINE DESIRES and DREAMS- What is my 'heart's desire'?

_____
_____
_____
_____

Picture your DREAMS as ALREADY FULFILLED-How does that FEEL?

_____
_____
_____
_____

POSITIVE INTENTION for TODAY- A Step toward my dreams!

_____
_____
_____
_____

What am I GRATEFUL for today?

_____

_____

_____

_____

I ACKNOWLEDGE SUCCESSES in myself and others!

_____

_____

_____

_____

DIVINE DESIRES and DREAMS- What is my 'heart's desire'?

_____

_____

_____

_____

Picture your DREAMS as ALREADY FULFILLED-How does that FEEL?

_____

_____

_____

_____

POSITIVE INTENTION for TODAY- A Step toward my dreams!

_____

_____

_____

_____

What am I GRATEFUL for today?

_____
_____
_____
_____

I ACKNOWLEDGE SUCCESSES in myself and others!

_____
_____
_____
_____

DIVINE DESIRES and DREAMS- What is my 'heart's desire'?

_____
_____
_____
_____

Picture your DREAMS as ALREADY FULFILLED-How does that FEEL?

_____
_____
_____
_____

POSITIVE INTENTION for TODAY- A Step toward my dreams!

_____
_____
_____
_____

What am I GRATEFUL for today?

_____
_____
_____
_____

I ACKNOWLEDGE SUCCESSES in myself and others!

_____
_____
_____
_____

DIVINE DESIRES and DREAMS- What is my 'heart's desire'?

_____
_____
_____
_____

Picture your DREAMS as ALREADY FULFILLED-How does that FEEL?

_____
_____
_____
_____

POSITIVE INTENTION for TODAY- A Step toward my dreams!

_____
_____
_____
_____

What am I GRATEFUL for today?   Date: _____

_____
_____
_____
_____

I ACKNOWLEDGE SUCCESSES in myself and others!

_____
_____
_____
_____

DIVINE DESIRES and DREAMS- What is my 'heart's desire'?

_____
_____
_____
_____

Picture your DREAMS as ALREADY FULFILLED-How does that FEEL?

_____
_____
_____
_____

POSITIVE INTENTION for TODAY- A Step toward my dreams!

_____
_____
_____
_____

What am I GRATEFUL for today?

_____

_____

_____

_____

I ACKNOWLEDGE SUCCESSES in myself and others!

_____

_____

_____

_____

DIVINE DESIRES and DREAMS- What is my 'heart's desire'?

_____

_____

_____

_____

Picture your DREAMS as ALREADY FULFILLED-How does that FEEL?

_____

_____

_____

_____

POSITIVE INTENTION for TODAY- A Step toward my dreams!

_____

_____

_____

_____

What am I GRATEFUL for today? Date: _____

_____
_____
_____
_____

I ACKNOWLEDGE SUCCESSES in myself and others!

_____
_____
_____
_____

DIVINE DESIRES and DREAMS- What is my 'heart's desire'?

_____
_____
_____
_____

Picture your DREAMS as ALREADY FULFILLED-How does that FEEL?

_____
_____
_____
_____

POSITIVE INTENTION for TODAY- A Step toward my dreams!

_____
_____
_____
_____

What am I GRATEFUL for today?

_____

_____

_____

_____

I ACKNOWLEDGE SUCCESSES in myself and others!

_____

_____

_____

_____

DIVINE DESIRES and DREAMS- What is my 'heart's desire'?

_____

_____

_____

_____

Picture your DREAMS as ALREADY FULFILLED-How does that FEEL?

_____

_____

_____

_____

POSITIVE INTENTION for TODAY- A Step toward my dreams!

_____

_____

_____

_____

What am I GRATEFUL for today?

_____
_____
_____
_____

I ACKNOWLEDGE SUCCESSES in myself and others!

_____
_____
_____
_____

DIVINE DESIRES and DREAMS- What is my 'heart's desire'?

_____
_____
_____
_____

Picture your DREAMS as ALREADY FULFILLED-How does that FEEL?

_____
_____
_____
_____

POSITIVE INTENTION for TODAY- A Step toward my dreams!

_____
_____
_____
_____

What am I GRATEFUL for today?

Date: _____

_____
_____
_____
_____

I ACKNOWLEDGE SUCCESSES in myself and others!

_____
_____
_____
_____

DIVINE DESIRES and DREAMS- What is my 'heart's desire'?

_____
_____
_____
_____

Picture your DREAMS as ALREADY FULFILLED-How does that FEEL?

_____
_____
_____
_____

POSITIVE INTENTION for TODAY- A Step toward my dreams!

_____
_____
_____
_____

What am I GRATEFUL for today?

_____
_____
_____
_____

I ACKNOWLEDGE SUCCESSES in myself and others!

_____
_____
_____
_____

DIVINE DESIRES and DREAMS- What is my 'heart's desire'?

_____
_____
_____
_____

Picture your DREAMS as ALREADY FULFILLED-How does that FEEL?

_____
_____
_____
_____

POSITIVE INTENTION for TODAY- A Step toward my dreams!

_____
_____
_____
_____

What am I GRATEFUL for today?

Date: _____

_____
_____
_____
_____

I ACKNOWLEDGE SUCCESSES in myself and others!

_____
_____
_____
_____

DIVINE DESIRES and DREAMS- What is my 'heart's desire'?

_____
_____
_____
_____

Picture your DREAMS as ALREADY FULFILLED-How does that FEEL?

_____
_____
_____
_____

POSITIVE INTENTION for TODAY- A Step toward my dreams!

_____
_____
_____
_____

What am I GRATEFUL for today?

_____
_____
_____
_____

I ACKNOWLEDGE SUCCESSES in myself and others!

_____
_____
_____
_____

DIVINE DESIRES and DREAMS- What is my 'heart's desire'?

_____
_____
_____
_____

Picture your DREAMS as ALREADY FULFILLED-How does that FEEL?

_____
_____
_____
_____

POSITIVE INTENTION for TODAY- A Step toward my dreams!

_____
_____
_____
_____

What am I GRATEFUL for today?

_____

_____

_____

_____

I ACKNOWLEDGE SUCCESSES in myself and others!

_____

_____

_____

_____

DIVINE DESIRES and DREAMS- What is my 'heart's desire'?

_____

_____

_____

_____

Picture your DREAMS as ALREADY FULFILLED-How does that FEEL?

_____

_____

_____

_____

POSITIVE INTENTION for TODAY- A Step toward my dreams!

_____

_____

_____

_____

What am I GRATEFUL for today?

_____
_____
_____
_____

I ACKNOWLEDGE SUCCESSES in myself and others!

_____
_____
_____
_____

DIVINE DESIRES and DREAMS- What is my 'heart's desire'?

_____
_____
_____
_____

Picture your DREAMS as ALREADY FULFILLED-How does that FEEL?

_____
_____
_____
_____

POSITIVE INTENTION for TODAY- A Step toward my dreams!

_____
_____
_____
_____

What am I GRATEFUL for today?

_____

_____

_____

_____

I ACKNOWLEDGE SUCCESSES in myself and others!

_____

_____

_____

_____

DIVINE DESIRES and DREAMS- What is my 'heart's desire'?

_____

_____

_____

_____

Picture your DREAMS as ALREADY FULFILLED-How does that FEEL?

_____

_____

_____

_____

POSITIVE INTENTION for TODAY- A Step toward my dreams!

_____

_____

_____

_____

What am I GRATEFUL for today?

_____
_____
_____
_____

I ACKNOWLEDGE SUCCESSES in myself and others!

_____
_____
_____
_____

DIVINE DESIRES and DREAMS- What is my 'heart's desire'?

_____
_____
_____
_____

Picture your DREAMS as ALREADY FULFILLED-How does that FEEL?

_____
_____
_____
_____

POSITIVE INTENTION for TODAY- A Step toward my dreams!

_____
_____
_____
_____

What am I GRATEFUL for today?   Date: _____

_____
_____
_____
_____

I ACKNOWLEDGE SUCCESSES in myself and others!

_____
_____
_____
_____

DIVINE DESIRES and DREAMS- What is my 'heart's desire'?

_____
_____
_____
_____

Picture your DREAMS as ALREADY FULFILLED-How does that FEEL?

_____
_____
_____
_____

POSITIVE INTENTION for TODAY- A Step toward my dreams!

_____
_____
_____
_____

What am I GRATEFUL for today?

_____
_____
_____
_____

I ACKNOWLEDGE SUCCESSES in myself and others!

_____
_____
_____
_____

DIVINE DESIRES and DREAMS- What is my 'heart's desire'?

_____
_____
_____
_____

Picture your DREAMS as ALREADY FULFILLED-How does that FEEL?

_____
_____
_____
_____

POSITIVE INTENTION for TODAY- A Step toward my dreams!

_____
_____
_____
_____

What am I GRATEFUL for today?

_____

_____

_____

_____

I ACKNOWLEDGE SUCCESSES in myself and others!

_____

_____

_____

_____

DIVINE DESIRES and DREAMS- What is my 'heart's desire'?

_____

_____

_____

_____

Picture your DREAMS as ALREADY FULFILLED-How does that FEEL?

_____

_____

_____

_____

POSITIVE INTENTION for TODAY- A Step toward my dreams!

_____

_____

_____

_____

What am I GRATEFUL for today?

_____
_____
_____
_____

I ACKNOWLEDGE SUCCESSES in myself and others!

_____
_____
_____
_____

DIVINE DESIRES and DREAMS- What is my 'heart's desire'?

_____
_____
_____
_____

Picture your DREAMS as ALREADY FULFILLED-How does that FEEL?

_____
_____
_____
_____

POSITIVE INTENTION for TODAY- A Step toward my dreams!

_____
_____
_____
_____

What am I GRATEFUL for today?

_____
_____
_____
_____

I ACKNOWLEDGE SUCCESSES in myself and others!

_____
_____
_____
_____

DIVINE DESIRES and DREAMS- What is my 'heart's desire'?

_____
_____
_____
_____

Picture your DREAMS as ALREADY FULFILLED-How does that FEEL?

_____
_____
_____
_____

POSITIVE INTENTION for TODAY- A Step toward my dreams!

_____
_____
_____
_____

What am I GRATEFUL for today?

_____
_____
_____
_____

I ACKNOWLEDGE SUCCESSES in myself and others!

_____
_____
_____
_____

DIVINE DESIRES and DREAMS- What is my 'heart's desire'?

_____
_____
_____
_____

Picture your DREAMS as ALREADY FULFILLED-How does that FEEL?

_____
_____
_____
_____

POSITIVE INTENTION for TODAY- A Step toward my dreams!

_____
_____
_____
_____

What am I GRATEFUL for today?   Date: _____

_____
_____
_____
_____

I ACKNOWLEDGE SUCCESSES in myself and others!

_____
_____
_____
_____

DIVINE DESIRES and DREAMS- What is my 'heart's desire'?

_____
_____
_____
_____

Picture your DREAMS as ALREADY FULFILLED-How does that FEEL?

_____
_____
_____
_____

POSITIVE INTENTION for TODAY- A Step toward my dreams!

_____
_____
_____
_____

What am I GRATEFUL for today?

_____

_____

_____

_____

I ACKNOWLEDGE SUCCESSES in myself and others!

_____

_____

_____

_____

DIVINE DESIRES and DREAMS- What is my 'heart's desire'?

_____

_____

_____

_____

Picture your DREAMS as ALREADY FULFILLED-How does that FEEL?

_____

_____

_____

_____

POSITIVE INTENTION for TODAY- A Step toward my dreams!

_____

_____

_____

_____

What am I GRATEFUL for today?

_____
_____
_____
_____

I ACKNOWLEDGE SUCCESSES in myself and others!

_____
_____
_____
_____

DIVINE DESIRES and DREAMS- What is my 'heart's desire'?

_____
_____
_____
_____

Picture your DREAMS as ALREADY FULFILLED-How does that FEEL?

_____
_____
_____
_____

POSITIVE INTENTION for TODAY- A Step toward my dreams!

_____
_____
_____
_____

What am I GRATEFUL for today?

Date: _____

I ACKNOWLEDGE SUCCESSES in myself and others!

DIVINE DESIRES and DREAMS- What is my 'heart's desire'?

Picture your DREAMS as ALREADY FULFILLED-How does that FEEL?

POSITIVE INTENTION for TODAY- A Step toward my dreams!

What am I GRATEFUL for today?

_____

_____

_____

_____

I ACKNOWLEDGE SUCCESSES in myself and others!

_____

_____

_____

_____

DIVINE DESIRES and DREAMS- What is my 'heart's desire'?

_____

_____

_____

_____

Picture your DREAMS as ALREADY FULFILLED-How does that FEEL?

_____

_____

_____

_____

POSITIVE INTENTION for TODAY- A Step toward my dreams!

_____

_____

_____

_____

What am I GRATEFUL for today?

Date: _____

_____

_____

_____

_____

I ACKNOWLEDGE SUCCESSES in myself and others!

_____

_____

_____

_____

DIVINE DESIRES and DREAMS- What is my 'heart's desire'?

_____

_____

_____

_____

Picture your DREAMS as ALREADY FULFILLED-How does that FEEL?

_____

_____

_____

_____

POSITIVE INTENTION for TODAY- A Step toward my dreams!

_____

_____

_____

_____

What am I GRATEFUL for today?

_____
_____
_____
_____

I ACKNOWLEDGE SUCCESSES in myself and others!

_____
_____
_____
_____

DIVINE DESIRES and DREAMS- What is my 'heart's desire'?

_____
_____
_____
_____

Picture your DREAMS as ALREADY FULFILLED-How does that FEEL?

_____
_____
_____
_____

POSITIVE INTENTION for TODAY- A Step toward my dreams!

_____
_____
_____
_____

What am I GRATEFUL for today?

_____
_____
_____
_____

I ACKNOWLEDGE SUCCESSES in myself and others!

_____
_____
_____
_____

DIVINE DESIRES and DREAMS- What is my 'heart's desire'?

_____
_____
_____
_____

Picture your DREAMS as ALREADY FULFILLED-How does that FEEL?

_____
_____
_____
_____

POSITIVE INTENTION for TODAY- A Step toward my dreams!

_____
_____
_____
_____

What am I GRATEFUL for today?

Date: _____

_____
_____
_____
_____

I ACKNOWLEDGE SUCCESSES in myself and others!

_____
_____
_____
_____

DIVINE DESIRES and DREAMS- What is my 'heart's desire'?

_____
_____
_____
_____

Picture your DREAMS as ALREADY FULFILLED-How does that FEEL?

_____
_____
_____
_____

POSITIVE INTENTION for TODAY- A Step toward my dreams!

_____
_____
_____
_____

What am I GRATEFUL for today?

_____
_____
_____
_____

I ACKNOWLEDGE SUCCESSES in myself and others!

_____
_____
_____
_____

DIVINE DESIRES and DREAMS- What is my 'heart's desire'?

_____
_____
_____
_____

Picture your DREAMS as ALREADY FULFILLED-How does that FEEL?

_____
_____
_____
_____

POSITIVE INTENTION for TODAY- A Step toward my dreams!

_____
_____
_____
_____

What am I GRATEFUL for today?

Date: _____

_____
_____
_____
_____

I ACKNOWLEDGE SUCCESSES in myself and others!

_____
_____
_____
_____

DIVINE DESIRES and DREAMS- What is my 'heart's desire'?

_____
_____
_____
_____

Picture your DREAMS as ALREADY FULFILLED-How does that FEEL?

_____
_____
_____
_____

POSITIVE INTENTION for TODAY- A Step toward my dreams!

_____
_____
_____
_____

What am I GRATEFUL for today?

_____

_____

_____

_____

I ACKNOWLEDGE SUCCESSES in myself and others!

_____

_____

_____

_____

DIVINE DESIRES and DREAMS- What is my 'heart's desire'?

_____

_____

_____

_____

Picture your DREAMS as ALREADY FULFILLED-How does that FEEL?

_____

_____

_____

_____

POSITIVE INTENTION for TODAY- A Step toward my dreams!

_____

_____

_____

_____

What am I GRATEFUL for today?

_____

_____

_____

_____

I ACKNOWLEDGE SUCCESSES in myself and others!

_____

_____

_____

_____

DIVINE DESIRES and DREAMS- What is my 'heart's desire'?

_____

_____

_____

_____

Picture your DREAMS as ALREADY FULFILLED-How does that FEEL?

_____

_____

_____

_____

POSITIVE INTENTION for TODAY- A Step toward my dreams!

_____

_____

_____

_____

What am I GRATEFUL for today?

_____
_____
_____
_____

I ACKNOWLEDGE SUCCESSES in myself and others!

_____
_____
_____
_____

DIVINE DESIRES and DREAMS- What is my 'heart's desire'?

_____
_____
_____
_____

Picture your DREAMS as ALREADY FULFILLED-How does that FEEL?

_____
_____
_____
_____

POSITIVE INTENTION for TODAY- A Step toward my dreams!

_____
_____
_____
_____

What am I GRATEFUL for today?

_____
_____
_____
_____

I ACKNOWLEDGE SUCCESSES in myself and others!

_____
_____
_____
_____

DIVINE DESIRES and DREAMS- What is my 'heart's desire'?

_____
_____
_____
_____

Picture your DREAMS as ALREADY FULFILLED-How does that FEEL?

_____
_____
_____
_____

POSITIVE INTENTION for TODAY- A Step toward my dreams!

_____
_____
_____
_____

What am I GRATEFUL for today?

_____
_____
_____
_____

I ACKNOWLEDGE SUCCESSES in myself and others!

_____
_____
_____
_____

DIVINE DESIRES and DREAMS- What is my 'heart's desire'?

_____
_____
_____
_____

Picture your DREAMS as ALREADY FULFILLED-How does that FEEL?

_____
_____
_____
_____

POSITIVE INTENTION for TODAY- A Step toward my dreams!

_____
_____
_____
_____

What am I GRATEFUL for today?

_____
_____
_____
_____

I ACKNOWLEDGE SUCCESSES in myself and others!

_____
_____
_____
_____

DIVINE DESIRES and DREAMS- What is my 'heart's desire'?

_____
_____
_____
_____

Picture your DREAMS as ALREADY FULFILLED-How does that FEEL?

_____
_____
_____
_____

POSITIVE INTENTION for TODAY- A Step toward my dreams!

_____
_____
_____
_____

What am I GRATEFUL for today?

Date: _____

_____
_____
_____
_____

I ACKNOWLEDGE SUCCESSES in myself and others!

_____
_____
_____
_____

DIVINE DESIRES and DREAMS- What is my 'heart's desire'?

_____
_____
_____
_____

Picture your DREAMS as ALREADY FULFILLED-How does that FEEL?

_____
_____
_____
_____

POSITIVE INTENTION for TODAY- A Step toward my dreams!

_____
_____
_____
_____

What am I GRATEFUL for today?

_____
_____
_____
_____

I ACKNOWLEDGE SUCCESSES in myself and others!

_____
_____
_____
_____

DIVINE DESIRES and DREAMS- What is my 'heart's desire'?

_____
_____
_____
_____

Picture your DREAMS as ALREADY FULFILLED-How does that FEEL?

_____
_____
_____
_____

POSITIVE INTENTION for TODAY- A Step toward my dreams!

_____
_____
_____
_____

What am I GRATEFUL for today?

Date: _____

_____
_____
_____
_____

I ACKNOWLEDGE SUCCESSES in myself and others!

_____
_____
_____
_____

DIVINE DESIRES and DREAMS- What is my 'heart's desire'?

_____
_____
_____
_____

Picture your DREAMS as ALREADY FULFILLED-How does that FEEL?

_____
_____
_____
_____

POSITIVE INTENTION for TODAY- A Step toward my dreams!

_____
_____
_____
_____

What am I GRATEFUL for today?   Date: _____

_____
_____
_____
_____

I ACKNOWLEDGE SUCCESSES in myself and others!

_____
_____
_____
_____

DIVINE DESIRES and DREAMS- What is my 'heart's desire'?

_____
_____
_____
_____

Picture your DREAMS as ALREADY FULFILLED-How does that FEEL?

_____
_____
_____
_____

POSITIVE INTENTION for TODAY- A Step toward my dreams!

_____
_____
_____
_____

What am I GRATEFUL for today?

Date: _____

_____
_____
_____
_____

I ACKNOWLEDGE SUCCESSES in myself and others!

_____
_____
_____
_____

DIVINE DESIRES and DREAMS- What is my 'heart's desire'?

_____
_____
_____
_____

Picture your DREAMS as ALREADY FULFILLED-How does that FEEL?

_____
_____
_____
_____

POSITIVE INTENTION for TODAY- A Step toward my dreams!

_____
_____
_____
_____

What am I GRATEFUL for today?

Date: _____

_____
_____
_____
_____

I ACKNOWLEDGE SUCCESSES in myself and others!

_____
_____
_____
_____

DIVINE DESIRES and DREAMS- What is my 'heart's desire'?

_____
_____
_____
_____

Picture your DREAMS as ALREADY FULFILLED-How does that FEEL?

_____
_____
_____
_____

POSITIVE INTENTION for TODAY- A Step toward my dreams!

_____
_____
_____
_____

What am I GRATEFUL for today?

_____
_____
_____
_____

I ACKNOWLEDGE SUCCESSES in myself and others!

_____
_____
_____
_____

DIVINE DESIRES and DREAMS- What is my 'heart's desire'?

_____
_____
_____
_____

Picture your DREAMS as ALREADY FULFILLED-How does that FEEL?

_____
_____
_____
_____

POSITIVE INTENTION for TODAY- A Step toward my dreams!

_____
_____
_____
_____

What am I GRATEFUL for today?   Date: _____

_____
_____
_____
_____

I ACKNOWLEDGE SUCCESSES in myself and others!

_____
_____
_____
_____

DIVINE DESIRES and DREAMS- What is my 'heart's desire'?

_____
_____
_____
_____

Picture your DREAMS as ALREADY FULFILLED-How does that FEEL?

_____
_____
_____
_____

POSITIVE INTENTION for TODAY- A Step toward my dreams!

_____
_____
_____
_____

What am I GRATEFUL for today?

Date: _____

I ACKNOWLEDGE SUCCESSES in myself and others!

_____
_____
_____
_____

DIVINE DESIRES and DREAMS- What is my 'heart's desire'?

_____
_____
_____
_____

Picture your DREAMS as ALREADY FULFILLED-How does that FEEL?

_____
_____
_____
_____

POSITIVE INTENTION for TODAY- A Step toward my dreams!

_____
_____
_____
_____

What am I GRATEFUL for today?

Date: _____

_____

_____

_____

_____

I ACKNOWLEDGE SUCCESSES in myself and others!

_____

_____

_____

_____

DIVINE DESIRES and DREAMS- What is my 'heart's desire'?

_____

_____

_____

_____

Picture your DREAMS as ALREADY FULFILLED-How does that FEEL?

_____

_____

_____

_____

POSITIVE INTENTION for TODAY- A Step toward my dreams!

_____

_____

_____

_____

What am I GRATEFUL for today?

_____
_____
_____
_____

I ACKNOWLEDGE SUCCESSES in myself and others!

_____
_____
_____
_____

DIVINE DESIRES and DREAMS- What is my 'heart's desire'?

_____
_____
_____
_____

Picture your DREAMS as ALREADY FULFILLED-How does that FEEL?

_____
_____
_____
_____

POSITIVE INTENTION for TODAY- A Step toward my dreams!

_____
_____
_____
_____

What am I GRATEFUL for today?

_____
_____
_____
_____

I ACKNOWLEDGE SUCCESSES in myself and others!

_____
_____
_____
_____

DIVINE DESIRES and DREAMS- What is my 'heart's desire'?

_____
_____
_____
_____

Picture your DREAMS as ALREADY FULFILLED-How does that FEEL?

_____
_____
_____
_____

POSITIVE INTENTION for TODAY- A Step toward my dreams!

_____
_____
_____
_____

What am I GRATEFUL for today?

_____
_____
_____
_____

I ACKNOWLEDGE SUCCESSES in myself and others!

_____
_____
_____
_____

DIVINE DESIRES and DREAMS- What is my 'heart's desire'?

_____
_____
_____
_____

Picture your DREAMS as ALREADY FULFILLED-How does that FEEL?

_____
_____
_____
_____

POSITIVE INTENTION for TODAY- A Step toward my dreams!

_____
_____
_____
_____

What am I GRATEFUL for today?

Date: _____

_____
_____
_____
_____

I ACKNOWLEDGE SUCCESSES in myself and others!

_____
_____
_____
_____

DIVINE DESIRES and DREAMS- What is my 'heart's desire'?

_____
_____
_____
_____

Picture your DREAMS as ALREADY FULFILLED-How does that FEEL?

_____
_____
_____
_____

POSITIVE INTENTION for TODAY- A Step toward my dreams!

_____
_____
_____
_____

What am I GRATEFUL for today?

Date: _____

_____
_____
_____
_____

I ACKNOWLEDGE SUCCESSES in myself and others!

_____
_____
_____
_____

DIVINE DESIRES and DREAMS- What is my 'heart's desire'?

_____
_____
_____
_____

Picture your DREAMS as ALREADY FULFILLED-How does that FEEL?

_____
_____
_____
_____

POSITIVE INTENTION for TODAY- A Step toward my dreams!

_____
_____
_____
_____

What am I GRATEFUL for today?   Date: _____

_____
_____
_____
_____

I ACKNOWLEDGE SUCCESSES in myself and others!

_____
_____
_____
_____

DIVINE DESIRES and DREAMS- What is my 'heart's desire'?

_____
_____
_____
_____

Picture your DREAMS as ALREADY FULFILLED-How does that FEEL?

_____
_____
_____
_____

POSITIVE INTENTION for TODAY- A Step toward my dreams!

_____
_____
_____
_____

What am I GRATEFUL for today?   Date: _____

_____
_____
_____
_____

I ACKNOWLEDGE SUCCESSES in myself and others!

_____
_____
_____
_____

DIVINE DESIRES and DREAMS- What is my 'heart's desire'?

_____
_____
_____
_____

Picture your DREAMS as ALREADY FULFILLED-How does that FEEL?

_____
_____
_____
_____

POSITIVE INTENTION for TODAY- A Step toward my dreams!

_____
_____
_____
_____

What am I GRATEFUL for today?

_____
_____
_____
_____

I ACKNOWLEDGE SUCCESSES in myself and others!

_____
_____
_____
_____

DIVINE DESIRES and DREAMS- What is my 'heart's desire'?

_____
_____
_____
_____

Picture your DREAMS as ALREADY FULFILLED-How does that FEEL?

_____
_____
_____
_____

POSITIVE INTENTION for TODAY- A Step toward my dreams!

_____
_____
_____
_____

What am I GRATEFUL for today?

_____
_____
_____
_____

I ACKNOWLEDGE SUCCESSES in myself and others!

_____
_____
_____
_____

DIVINE DESIRES and DREAMS- What is my 'heart's desire'?

_____
_____
_____
_____

Picture your DREAMS as ALREADY FULFILLED-How does that FEEL?

_____
_____
_____
_____

POSITIVE INTENTION for TODAY- A Step toward my dreams!

_____
_____
_____
_____

What am I GRATEFUL for today?

Date: _____

_____
_____
_____
_____

I ACKNOWLEDGE SUCCESSES in myself and others!

_____
_____
_____
_____

DIVINE DESIRES and DREAMS- What is my 'heart's desire'?

_____
_____
_____
_____

Picture your DREAMS as ALREADY FULFILLED-How does that FEEL?

_____
_____
_____
_____

POSITIVE INTENTION for TODAY- A Step toward my dreams!

_____
_____
_____
_____

What am I GRATEFUL for today?

_____
_____
_____
_____

I ACKNOWLEDGE SUCCESSES in myself and others!

_____
_____
_____
_____

DIVINE DESIRES and DREAMS- What is my 'heart's desire'?

_____
_____
_____
_____

Picture your DREAMS as ALREADY FULFILLED-How does that FEEL?

_____
_____
_____
_____

POSITIVE INTENTION for TODAY- A Step toward my dreams!

_____
_____
_____
_____

What am I GRATEFUL for today?

_____

_____

_____

_____

I ACKNOWLEDGE SUCCESSES in myself and others!

_____

_____

_____

_____

DIVINE DESIRES and DREAMS- What is my 'heart's desire'?

_____

_____

_____

_____

Picture your DREAMS as ALREADY FULFILLED-How does that FEEL?

_____

_____

_____

_____

POSITIVE INTENTION for TODAY- A Step toward my dreams!

_____

_____

_____

_____

What am I GRATEFUL for today?

_____
_____
_____
_____

I ACKNOWLEDGE SUCCESSES in myself and others!

_____
_____
_____
_____

DIVINE DESIRES and DREAMS- What is my 'heart's desire'?

_____
_____
_____
_____

Picture your DREAMS as ALREADY FULFILLED-How does that FEEL?

_____
_____
_____
_____

POSITIVE INTENTION for TODAY- A Step toward my dreams!

_____
_____
_____
_____

What am I GRATEFUL for today?

_____
_____
_____
_____

I ACKNOWLEDGE SUCCESSES in myself and others!

_____
_____
_____
_____

DIVINE DESIRES and DREAMS- What is my 'heart's desire'?

_____
_____
_____
_____

Picture your DREAMS as ALREADY FULFILLED-How does that FEEL?

_____
_____
_____
_____

POSITIVE INTENTION for TODAY- A Step toward my dreams!

_____
_____
_____
_____

What am I GRATEFUL for today?

_____
_____
_____
_____

I ACKNOWLEDGE SUCCESSES in myself and others!

_____
_____
_____
_____

DIVINE DESIRES and DREAMS- What is my 'heart's desire'?

_____
_____
_____
_____

Picture your DREAMS as ALREADY FULFILLED-How does that FEEL?

_____
_____
_____
_____

POSITIVE INTENTION for TODAY- A Step toward my dreams!

_____
_____
_____
_____

What am I GRATEFUL for today?

_____

_____

_____

_____

I ACKNOWLEDGE SUCCESSES in myself and others!

_____

_____

_____

_____

DIVINE DESIRES and DREAMS- What is my 'heart's desire'?

_____

_____

_____

_____

Picture your DREAMS as ALREADY FULFILLED-How does that FEEL?

_____

_____

_____

_____

POSITIVE INTENTION for TODAY- A Step toward my dreams!

_____

_____

_____

_____

What am I GRATEFUL for today?

_____
_____
_____
_____

I ACKNOWLEDGE SUCCESSES in myself and others!

_____
_____
_____
_____

DIVINE DESIRES and DREAMS- What is my 'heart's desire'?

_____
_____
_____
_____

Picture your DREAMS as ALREADY FULFILLED-How does that FEEL?

_____
_____
_____
_____

POSITIVE INTENTION for TODAY- A Step toward my dreams!

_____
_____
_____
_____

What am I GRATEFUL for today? Date: _____

_____
_____
_____
_____

I ACKNOWLEDGE SUCCESSES in myself and others!

_____
_____
_____
_____

DIVINE DESIRES and DREAMS- What is my 'heart's desire'?

_____
_____
_____
_____

Picture your DREAMS as ALREADY FULFILLED-How does that FEEL?

_____
_____
_____
_____

POSITIVE INTENTION for TODAY- A Step toward my dreams!

_____
_____
_____
_____

What am I GRATEFUL for today?

_____
_____
_____
_____

I ACKNOWLEDGE SUCCESSES in myself and others!

_____
_____
_____
_____

DIVINE DESIRES and DREAMS- What is my 'heart's desire'?

_____
_____
_____
_____

Picture your DREAMS as ALREADY FULFILLED-How does that FEEL?

_____
_____
_____
_____

POSITIVE INTENTION for TODAY- A Step toward my dreams!

_____
_____
_____
_____